Jeff can't wait for the lesson to finish. He turns to Jazz and sighs.

... Pegasus had wings ...
Jeff!

Back on the sand, the Rockets finish playing football. The girls win!
Wicked goal, Jazz!
All down to teamwork!

O.K., now I'm going to chill in the sun.

Jazz is soon asleep in the warm sun!

She dreams that the match is sold out.

It's Pegasus! Jazz and Mel rush to get on its back!

Soon they are high in the air!

Up so high on Pegasus,
they can see the game.
They don't need tickets now!

All of a sudden the dream, and Pegasus, vanish! Jazz has been hit with a ball!

We are off to see the Sunset Rockets!
But we can't go. They are full!
Yes we can! We've got tickets!

Jazz can't wait to go! She had just been dreaming!
Red hair ... ?
But was she?!